BOWL GAMES OF COLLEGE FOOTBALL

THE STORY OF THE SUGAR BOWL

by Will Graves

SportsZone
An Imprint of Abdo Publishing | abdopublishing.com

abdopublishing.com

Published by Abdo Publishing, a division of ABDO, PO Box 398166, Minneapolis, Minnesota 55439. Copyright © 2016 by Abdo Consulting Group, Inc. International copyrights reserved in all countries. No part of this book may be reproduced in any form without written permission from the publisher. SportsZone™ is a trademark and logo of Abdo Publishing.

Printed in the United States of America, North Mankato, Minnesota
052015
092015

THIS BOOK CONTAINS RECYCLED MATERIALS

Cover Photos: Dave Martin/AP Images
Interior Images: Dave Martin/AP Images, 1, 38; AP Images, 4, 6, 8, 10, 14, 16, 20, 23, 24, 29, 30, 32; Bill Allen/AP Images, 12; Rich Clarkson/Sports Illustrated/Getty Images, 18; Bill Feig/AP Images, 26; A.J. Sisco/UPI Photo Service/Newscom, 35; Rico Clements/UPI Photo Service/Newscom, 36; Bill Haber/AP Images, 40, 42; David J. Phillip/AP Images, 43
Editor: Patrick Donnelly
Series Designer: Nikki Farinella

Library of Congress Control Number: 2015931667

Cataloging-in-Publication Data
Graves, Will.
 The story of the Sugar Bowl / Will Graves.
   p. cm. -- (Bowl games of college football)
Includes bibliographical references and index.
ISBN 978-1-62403-891-4
1. Sugar Bowl (Football game)--History--Juvenile literature. 2. Football--United States--Juvenile literature. 3. College sports--Juvenile literature. I. Title.
796.332--dc23
                                                                              2015931667

TABLE OF CONTENTS

1. **Sugar Bowl History: A Sweet Idea** 5
2. **1951: Bear's Secret Weapon (Kentucky vs. Oklahoma)** 9
3. **1973: Pluck of the Irish (Notre Dame vs. Alabama)** 15
4. **1977: Perfect Panthers (Pittsburgh vs. Georgia)** 21
5. **1983: No-Nonsense Champs (Penn State vs. Georgia)** 27
6. **2000: Age Before Beauty (Florida State vs. Virginia Tech)** 33
7. **2010: Tebow Time (Florida vs. Cincinnati)** 39

Timeline 42
Bowl Records 44
Quotes and Anecdotes 45
Glossary 46
For More Information 47
Index/About the Author 48

Alabama players carry coach Paul "Bear" Bryant off the field after beating Nebraska 34–7 in the 1967 Sugar Bowl.

SUGAR BOWL HISTORY:
A SWEET IDEA

In the early days of college football, there was only one bowl game.

First played in 1902 (though it did not become an annual event until 1916), the Rose Bowl gave two schools an opportunity to play one more game in warm and sunny Southern California. And it was more than just a game—it was a week-long party for the teams and their fans.

Other cities noticed the wave of visitors who traveled to support their teams. In New Orleans, Louisiana, two local newspapermen thought it was time for the city called "The Big Easy" to get in on the act.

Colonel James M. Thompson and Fred Digby both worked at the *New Orleans Item* newspaper in the

Louisiana State halfback Abe Mickal breaks through the line of scrimmage against Texas Christian in the second Sugar Bowl, played on January 1, 1936, at Tulane Stadium.

1920s. Thompson was the publisher. Digby worked on the sports section. They wanted to invite two top teams to face each other on New Year's Day at Tulane Stadium in New Orleans. Digby thought the name "Sugar Bowl" would help the game stand out. Louisiana is one of the top sugar-producing states in the United States. Digby also came up with a list of activities to go along with the game, from a track meet to a rowing competition to a tennis tournament.

The first Sugar Bowl was played in 1935. It soon became one of the hottest tickets in sports. By 1939, Tulane Stadium expanded to hold more fans. By the 1950s, more than 80,000 people came each year to watch two of college football's best teams face off.

What started as a yearly showdown usually between teams from the South grew. Soon, schools from all over the country wanted to spend New Year's in New Orleans.

Over the years, the game became more important. It moved from Tulane Stadium to the Superdome in 1975, and the party just kept getting bigger.

The Most Valuable Player (MVP) of each Sugar Bowl wins the Miller-Digby Trophy. It is named for Warren Miller, who was the first president of the Sugar Bowl, and Digby, the man who thought having a bowl game in New Orleans would be a pretty sweet idea. He was right. And then some.

NOT JUST FOOTBALL

Sugar Bowl officials had more than just football in mind when they created the bowl game. They used the game to promote other athletic events, too. One such event is the Sugar Bowl Classic basketball game. For years, it was one of the best regular-season college basketball events on the calendar. In the mid-2000s the event changed to a high school basketball tournament for top teams from all over the country.

Kentucky coach Paul "Bear" Bryant plots strategy with quarterback Babe Parilli at a practice before the 1951 Sugar Bowl.

1951
BEAR'S SECRET WEAPON
Kentucky vs. Oklahoma

Paul Bryant was a teenager growing up in southern Arkansas in the 1920s when, according to legend, he heard about a way to make a quick buck. All Bryant had to do was wrestle a bear. If he could beat the bear, he would win a dollar.

Bryant won. The bear's owner did not pay up, but Bryant earned something more important than money that day. His friends gave him the nickname "Bear" after the match, and a legend was born.

"Bear" Bryant played football as a youth and at the University of Alabama, but he moved into coaching after graduating in 1936. He worked his way up the ranks as an assistant and became the head coach at the

Oklahoma coach Bud Wilkinson, *center*, meets with his defense as they prepare to face Kentucky in the 1951 Sugar Bowl.

University of Maryland in 1945, even though he was barely a decade older than most of his players.

Bryant stayed at Maryland for one season, then returned to the South to take over the program at the University of Kentucky. It did not take long for the tough and driven Bryant to turn the Wildcats into winners. He guided Kentucky to a 10-1 record in 1950 to win the Southeastern Conference (SEC) title. They earned a spot in the Sugar Bowl against the unbeaten Oklahoma Sooners, the top-ranked team in the country.

The Wildcats were heavy underdogs to the mighty Sooners. Coach Bud Wilkinson had put together a team that steamrolled opponents. Oklahoma won its 10 regular season games by an average of 21 points. They were led by halfback Billy Vessels, who scored 15 touchdowns, and fullback Leon "Mule Train" Heath.

Back then, the final rankings came out before the bowl games. So by the time Kentucky and Oklahoma met on January 1, 1951, the Sooners had already been declared the national champions.

Kentucky and Bryant had other ideas. Bryant was one of the most inventive coaches in football history, and he created a scheme to slow down Oklahoma's "go-go" offense. Instead of using three defensive linemen, as most teams did, Bryant added a fourth man on the line to stop the Sooners' running game.

The fourth defensive lineman was Walt Yowarsky. Bryant moved the 6-foot-2-inch (1.88-m), 208-pound (94-kg) Yowarsky from offense to defense before the game. Bryant hoped Yowarsky's size would help put the brakes on Vessels and Heath.

It worked to perfection. Yowarsky recovered a fumble by Oklahoma quarterback Claude Arnold on the Sooners' first offensive play. The Wildcats scored a touchdown to take an early lead. Yowarsky later stuffed Arnold for a 12-yard loss to set up another Kentucky score to make it 13–0.

Kentucky's Babe Parilli, *right*, tries to escape an Oklahoma defender in the 1951 Sugar Bowl.

The Sooners pulled within 13-7 with six minutes left in the game. Then they stopped the Wildcats to get the ball back with a chance to win. Yowarsky was not about to let that happen. Bryant's secret weapon made one last big play. Yowarsky recovered a fumble by Oklahoma's Jake Lockett in the final moments to help Kentucky pull off the upset in front of 80,000 fans.

Bryant would go on to become one of the greatest coaches in college football history. He left Kentucky for Texas A&M in 1954, then he moved to Alabama in 1958. Bryant won six national championships at his alma mater and captured seven more Sugar Bowls.

No Sugar Bowl, though, may have been as important as his first. That was when the coach who earned his toughness by fighting a bear helped a team full of Wildcats take down the national champions.

HOW LOW CAN YOU GO?

The weather during the early years of the Sugar Bowl often made for difficult playing conditions. The 1942 game may have been the worst of all. Playing in a rainstorm that made it difficult to see, Fordham edged Missouri 2–0. The Rams blocked a punt for a safety for the game's only score.

Alabama's Wilbur Jackson, *back*, loses the football after a hard hit by Notre Dame's Reggie Barnett in the 1973 Sugar Bowl.

1973
PLUCK OF THE IRISH
Notre Dame vs. Alabama

Notre Dame had a choice after going undefeated during the 1973 regular season. The Fighting Irish, one of college football's top programs, could play in the Orange Bowl or the Sugar Bowl. The Orange Bowl in Miami offered more money. The Sugar Bowl offered an opportunity to play top-ranked Alabama.

The Irish opted for a trip to New Orleans, giving the Sugar Bowl a matchup of two unbeaten teams for the first time in its history.

Even though Alabama and Notre Dame had long been national powers, they had never faced each other. That all changed on a gusty night at Tulane Stadium on December 31, 1973. More than 85,000 people packed

Notre Dame players carry head coach Ara Parseghian off the field after completing an undefeated season with a 24-23 victory over Alabama in the 1973 Sugar Bowl.

Tulane Stadium, with millions more watching on TV to see who would win this battle of giants.

The Crimson Tide and coach Paul "Bear" Bryant had rolled to a perfect 11-0 record during the regular season. No opponent had come within 14 points of Alabama. Notre Dame and coach Ara Parseghian also went undefeated, but its road to a perfect record was tougher. The Irish ended Southern Cal's 23-game unbeaten streak in October with a dramatic 23-14 victory. They stayed hot the rest of the year and were still riding high as they headed to New Orleans.

Alabama was favored by a touchdown, but a thunderstorm hours before kickoff made the artificial turf slick. Both teams switched to the shoes used by Tulane's players to keep from slipping. The soggy conditions gave both offenses an advantage as the defenses tried to keep up.

Notre Dame took a 14–10 halftime lead thanks to a 93-yard kickoff return for a touchdown by Al Hunter. Alabama then rallied to move ahead in the fourth quarter thanks to a gamble that paid off for Bryant.

Running back Mike Stock and backup quarterback Richard Todd entered the game. Todd took the snap and pitched the ball to Stock, who ran to his right. Then as the Irish defense closed in, he pulled up to pass. Stock managed to get the throw off before getting crushed by several players. The ball floated to a wide-open Todd, who trotted into the end zone for a 25-yard touchdown to put Alabama ahead 23–21. Another Sugar Bowl win and national title for Alabama appeared to be within reach.

Notre Dame fought back to move in front 24–23 on a 19-yard field goal by Bob Thomas with 4:12 left. Alabama had to punt, but the Crimson Tide downed the ball at the Notre Dame 1. With his team's back against

Notre Dame quarterback Tom Clements, 2, fires a deep pass to wide receiver Robin Weber for a crucial first down late in the 1973 Sugar Bowl against Alabama.

the wall, Parseghian showed that Bryant was not the only coach who could take a major risk.

Facing third-and-9 from their own 2-yard line with less than 3 minutes to play, Parseghian called for a pass. Irish quarterback Tom Clements rolled to his left. His favorite target, tight end Dave Casper, was covered, but Clements spied Robin Weber out of the corner of his eye. Weber had not caught a ball all season and had missed two days of practice leading up to the game.

Still, Weber was open. Clements fired a perfect strike to the surprised wide receiver, who hauled it in for a 36-yard gain. Notre Dame then ran out the clock to hand Bryant the only Sugar Bowl defeat of his career. The Irish and Crimson Tide split the votes in the national championship polls, so they officially shared the title that year.

"There were no losers in that game," Parseghian said.

He was right. And the biggest winner might have been the Sugar Bowl itself.

COLLEGE FOOTBALL PLAYOFF

In 2014, the highest level of college football adopted a new playoff system. A committee now determines the nation's four best teams for a playoff. The semifinal games rotate between six major bowl games each year. The Sugar Bowl is one of those six bowls. It hosted a national semifinal game on January 1, 2015. Fourth-seeded Ohio State shocked top-ranked Alabama 42–35 to earn a trip to the national championship game. Under the new plan, the Sugar Bowl will be a national semifinal game once every three years.

Running back Tony Dorsett of Pittsburgh breaks through an attempted tackle by Georgia's Johnny Henderson in the 1977 Sugar Bowl.

1977
PERFECT
PANTHERS
Pittsburgh vs. Georgia

By the mid-1970s, the Sugar Bowl had a new home and an official host. Officials moved the game from the aging Tulane Stadium to the brand-new Superdome in 1975. The massive stadium was home to the NFL's Saints and closer to downtown New Orleans. The modern dome meant weather was no longer an issue for fans. The stadium's Astroturf field also made for a faster, more exciting game.

But that was not the only new wrinkle. The Sugar Bowl worked out a deal with the SEC, awarding one of the bowl berths to its champion each year. Georgia steamrolled its way to the SEC title in 1976 behind a defense nicknamed the "Junkyard Dogs." They were a nasty, hard-hitting bunch. The players shaved their heads as proof of their toughness. Coach Vince Dooley promised the Bulldogs if they won the SEC he would shave his head, too. He could only smile when his players broke out the razor after the Bulldogs went 10-1 during the regular season to capture the conference title and earn a trip to New Orleans.

Top-ranked and unbeaten Pittsburgh awaited Georgia at the Superdome. The Panthers went 11-0 in 1976 behind electric running back Tony Dorsett. The senior set a National Collegiate Athletic Association (NCAA) record with 2,150 yards rushing that season. He easily won the Heisman Trophy, given to the best player in college football.

Pitt's rise to the top began three years earlier, when coach Johnny Majors took over an average program and molded it into a champion. With Majors calling the shots and Dorsett running wild, the Panthers were nearly unstoppable in 1976. They breezed through the regular season. Only rival West Virginia lost by fewer than 10 points against the Panthers. Pitt won 24-16 in its closest game of the year.

Georgia came up with a plan to slow down Dorsett. The Bulldogs put together a 6-2 defense that put six defensive linemen at the line of scrimmage. The plan

As the Panthers mascot cheers, Pittsburgh quarterback Matt Cavanaugh, *top*, celebrates his first-quarter touchdown run against Georgia in the 1977 Sugar Bowl. Willie Taylor, *left*, and Tony Dorsett congratulate him.

was to take away any running room for Dorsett and dare the Panthers to beat them by passing the ball.

Pitt quarterback Matt Cavanaugh was up to the challenge. Cavanaugh carved up the "Junkyard Dogs" on the second Panther drive, hitting Elliot Walker for a 36-yard gain that put Pitt in scoring position. Cavanaugh gave Pitt an early lead with a 6-yard touchdown run. He then hit Gordon Jones for a 59-yard strike that made it 14–0 in the second quarter.

Cavanaugh was so successful that Georgia was forced to stop focusing on Dorsett. That did not work either. Dorsett made it 21–0 just before halftime when

Pittsburgh coach Johnny Majors carries the Sugar Bowl trophy off the field after his team won the national championship by whipping Georgia 27–3.

he scored on an 11-yard run. And he was just getting started. Dorsett darted over, around, and through the Bulldogs in the second half as Pitt controlled the clock and the game. Dorsett rolled up 137 of his 202 yards rushing in the second half as the Panthers cruised to a 27–3 victory.

Cavanaugh narrowly beat out Dorsett for the game's MVP, though the real star was Majors. The coach who turned the Panthers into champions raised his index finger and made the "number-one" sign when the final gun sounded. His players had left no doubt they were the best team in the nation.

It turned out to be Majors's final game at Pitt. He left to take the job at Tennessee, his alma mater. His parting gift to the Panthers was a perfect 12–0 season that capped one of the most successful rebuilding projects in college football history.

ON THE ROAD

The Sugar Bowl is a yearly event in New Orleans, but the 2006 game was moved to Atlanta when the Superdome was damaged during a hurricane. It turned into a homecoming of sorts for Georgia. But playing just a short drive from its campus did not help. The Bulldogs could not keep up with West Virginia. The Mountaineers raced to a 38–35 victory behind 382 rushing yards.

Penn State coach Joe Paterno waves to the crowd as he is carried off the field by his players after the Nittany Lions won their first national title by beating Georgia in the 1983 Sugar Bowl.

1983 NO-NONSENSE CHAMPS
Penn State vs. Georgia

Penn State coach Joe Paterno was a straitlaced kind of guy. He wore thick glasses, a blue or white shirt, a tie, dress pants, and black shoes with white socks just about every day.

Paterno's teams looked a lot like their coach. The Nittany Lions had plain white helmets. They wore navy blue and white jerseys. There were no stripes on their shoulders and no names on their backs. The way they played was just as simple. Paterno molded Penn State into a national power behind a tough defense and an offense that relied on the running game.

Paterno took over as coach at Penn State in 1966. The wins soon started to pile up, but all those regular-season victories failed to bring a national title.

Penn State went undefeated in 1968, 1969, and 1973 but did not finish atop the polls in any of those seasons. The Nittany Lions came close in 1978, when they lost to Alabama 14–7 in the Sugar Bowl after the Crimson Tide made a dramatic goal-line stand.

The Nittany Lions were not expected to compete for a championship in 1982. Alabama blew them out 42–21 in October, but Penn State rallied. It rose to number two in the polls and beat rival Pittsburgh 19–10 in the season finale to earn a trip to the Sugar Bowl. The reward? A game against the best running back and the best team in the country.

Georgia star Herschel Walker was not just a football player—he was a force of nature. At 6 feet 1 inch (1.85 m) tall and weighing 225 pounds (102 kg), Walker was more like a tank than a running back. He was strong enough to run over defenders and fast enough to run by them. He did plenty of both in 1982, his junior year at Georgia. Walker captured the Heisman Trophy that year. He rushed for 1,752 yards and 16 touchdowns even though he fractured his right thumb just two weeks before the season opener.

With Walker leading the way, the Bulldogs went 11–0 and headed to New Orleans with a chance to win their

Georgia running back Herschel Walker breaks through a would-be Penn State tackler during the 1983 Sugar Bowl.

second national championship in three years. Only second-ranked Penn State and Paterno stood in the way.

The battle between the nation's two top teams proved to be worth the wait. The Nittany Lions raced to a 20–3 lead behind running back Curt Warner and quarterback Todd Blackledge. But Georgia clawed its way back. Though Penn State kept Walker mostly bottled up, the Bulldogs pulled to within 20–17 in the third quarter when the Heisman winner plowed into the end zone from a yard out.

Paterno could feel another chance at the national title slipping away. He decided it was not time to play

Penn State wide receiver Gregg Garrity makes a diving catch for a touchdown that helped clinch the 1983 Sugar Bowl against Georgia.

it safe. With the ball near midfield, Blackledge called "six-43." The play called for Blackledge to fake a handoff to Warner then look for a wide receiver streaking downfield.

It worked to perfection. Blackledge flung the ball down the sideline as Gregg Garrity broke free. Garrity made a spectacular diving grab as he flew over the goal line. The touchdown gave the Nittany Lions a 27–17 advantage. Georgia scored late to make it 27–23, but Penn State ran out the clock.

Warner ran for 177 yards and two touchdowns, far more than Walker, who needed 28 carries to run for 103 yards and a score. Blackledge won the Miller-Digby Award as the game's MVP, but the brightest spotlight was on Paterno. After more than 15 years at Penn State, the no-nonsense coach was a champion, white socks and all.

A SPECIAL HOST

The Rose Bowl has the Southern California sun. The Orange Bowl has tropical breezes. The Sugar Bowl has the Superdome. The gigantic stadium is as much a part of the game as marching bands and New Year's Day. The 72,000-seat dome had a makeover following Hurricane Katrina in 2005, meaning the Sugar Bowl will have a state-of-the-art home for years to come.

Florida State wide receiver Peter Warrick, *right*, catches a touchdown pass as Virginia Tech's Ronyell Whitaker tries to defend in the 2000 Sugar Bowl.

2000
AGE BEFORE BEAUTY
Florida State vs. Virginia Tech

College football had never seen anything like Michael Vick. Virginia Tech's freshman quarterback had the speed of a wide receiver, the shifty moves of a running back, and a powerful left arm that could fling the ball 60 yards with ease.

College football had never seen anything quite like Chris Weinke, either. The Florida State quarterback spent six years playing minor league baseball after high school before going to college. By the time he joined the Seminoles, he was in his mid-20s, and he turned 27 before the 1999 season. He was nearly a decade older than some of his teammates.

Vick and Weinke both led their teams to 11–0 records in the 1999 regular season. They just did it in different ways. Vick was electric. He could break off a long touchdown run or flick his wrist and hit a Hokies wide receiver racing downfield.

Weinke was the opposite. He would stand in the pocket in the face of the pass rush and look for one of his playmakers. There were plenty to go around for the Seminoles that year. Wide receiver Peter Warrick was one of the best players in the country. The running game had shifty Travis Minor and powerful Dan Kendra.

The Seminoles started the season as the top-ranked team and never gave up their spot. The Hokies began the year ranked eleventh and quickly climbed to second with Vick leading the way. The only two undefeated teams left at the end of the regular season were set up for a showdown at the Superdome.

The game produced plenty of fireworks. Florida State took a 28–7 lead and looked as though it would blow the Hokies all the way back to Virginia. Warrick had hauled in a 64-yard touchdown pass from Weinke to start the scoring. Warrick later returned a punt 59 yards for another score. He zigzagged his way to the end zone, and the Seminoles were up by three touchdowns before the game was 20 minutes old.

But Vick did not panic. Neither did his teammates. Slicing his way through Florida State's stout defense,

Virginia Tech quarterback Michael Vick gets swallowed up by the Florida State defense during the 2000 Sugar Bowl.

the young quarterback led a comeback. Virginia Tech reeled off 22 straight points to take a 29–28 lead into the fourth quarter.

The Seminoles responded like champions. Weinke found wide receiver Ron Dugans for a 14-yard score to put Florida State back in front. Sebastian Janikowski hit a short field goal, and Warrick ended his record day with a 43-yard scoring grab.

35

Quarterback Chris Weinke gets a hug from a Seminoles cheerleader after Florida State clinched a national championship with a 46–29 victory over Virginia Tech in the 2000 Sugar Bowl.

Florida State sealed its national title with a 46–29 win. Warrick won the Miller-Digby Award after scoring a then-record 20 points on three touchdowns and a two-point conversion. Weinke passed for 329 yards and four scores.

> **TOUGH TICKET**
>
> It cost just $1.50 to get into Tulane Stadium for the first Sugar Bowl in 1936. Prices have gone up—way up—ever since. Although tickets for the 2015 Sugar Bowl started at $45, the closest seats cost $300 or more. No matter the price, people will pay. The Sugar Bowl is sold out every year.

Vick was every bit Weinke's match. He threw for 225 yards and a touchdown and ran for 97 yards and a score. It was a spectacular day for a freshman. It just was not quite good enough to knock off the Seminoles as coach Bobby Bowden won his second national title.

"It's a load off your shoulders to win this one," Bowden said. "This one I can enjoy."

Florida quarterback Tim Tebow runs for a first down against Cincinnati in the 2010 Sugar Bowl.

2010
TEBOW TIME
Florida vs. Cincinnati

Tim Tebow made history during his four years at the University of Florida. In 2007 he became the first sophomore to win the Heisman Trophy. Tebow was more than a quarterback. He was a fullback who could bowl over tacklers. And he was a passer whose funky left-armed delivery still found a way to get the job done.

Mostly though, Tebow was a winner. He split time at quarterback as a freshman. The Gators beat Ohio State in the Bowl Championship Series (BCS) National Championship Game that year. Tebow started the next three seasons, and Florida's success continued. The Gators went back to the BCS title game in 2008 and

Florida fans demonstrate their support for Tim Tebow and the Gators at the 2010 Sugar Bowl.

knocked off Oklahoma. They went 48-7 in Tebow's four years on campus.

Everywhere Tebow went, people followed. "Tebowmania" swept the nation. On the first day of 2010, the show finally came to the Sugar Bowl.

The Gators started the season ranked number one. And they stayed there until the SEC championship game, where they lost to rival Alabama. Although the Crimson Tide went on to the BCS title game, Florida took its star quarterback to New Orleans for the Sugar Bowl.

Cincinnati, the Big East Conference champion, was eager to see Tebow up close. The Bearcats were undefeated during the regular season, having won all 12 of their games. Their offense put up numbers that would have been hard to duplicate on a video game. Cincinnati averaged 39.8 points per game and even put up 70 points on Southeast Missouri State. A win over Florida would prove the Bearcats were the real deal.

The Gators had other plans. Tebow connected on his first 12 passes, most of them short tosses that his receivers turned into big plays. By the end of the first half, Tebow was 20-for-23 for 320 yards and three touchdowns. That was more passing yards than Tebow had during an entire game all season.

He was not finished. Not by a long shot. The Gators, angry they missed out on a shot at the national title, took it out on the Bearcats. Florida poured it on well into the second half, adding three more scores in a 51–24 romp.

Tebow finished the last game of his college career going 31-for-35 for a Sugar Bowl record 482 yards and three touchdowns. He ran for 51 yards and another touchdown. His 533 yards of total offense was the most ever by a player in a major bowl game.

TIMELINE

1934
The New Orleans Mid-Winter Sports Association, the group that organized the first Sugar Bowl, is formed.

1935
Tulane beats Temple 20–14 in front of 22,026 at Tulane Stadium in the inaugural Sugar Bowl game.

1936
Pittsburgh edges defending national champion Louisiana State (LSU) 52–47 in the first Sugar Bowl basketball game.

1939
Interest in the game grows so rapidly that officials call for a plan to expand seating at Tulane Stadium to 70,000.

1942
Fordham edges Missouri 2–0 in the lowest-scoring Sugar Bowl ever.

1947
Officials create the Warren V. Miller Memorial Trophy (later renamed the Miller-Digby Memorial Trophy), given each year to the Sugar Bowl's most outstanding player.

1953
The Sugar Bowl is televised for the first time as number three Georgia Tech beats sixth-ranked Mississippi 24–7.

1971
Secretary of Defense Melvin Laird attends the game to watch fourth-ranked Tennessee knock off the Air Force Academy 34–13.

1972
A record crowd of 84,031 shows up at Tulane Stadium to watch Oklahoma top Auburn 40–22.

1972
On New Year's Eve, number two Oklahoma blanks fifth-ranked Penn State 14–0 in the first Sugar Bowl played at night.

1975
Alabama edges Penn State 13–6 on New Year's Eve in the first Sugar Bowl played in the Superdome.

1984
Auburn tops Michigan 9–7 in the fiftieth Sugar Bowl.

1997
Florida avenges an earlier loss to Florida State and crushes the Seminoles 52–20 to win the national title.

2002
LSU beats Illinois 47–34 in the highest-scoring Sugar Bowl ever.

2004
LSU upsets Oklahoma 21–14 in front of a Superdome record crowd of 79,342 to win the national championship.

2005
Hurricane Katrina causes major damage to the Superdome. Sugar Bowl officials decide weeks later to move the 2006 game to Atlanta.

2015
Fourth-ranked Ohio State upsets number one Alabama 42–35 in the semifinals of the first-ever College Football Playoff.

43

BOWL RECORDS

Most appearances by one school
15, Alabama

Most victories by one school
8, Alabama

Most losses by one school
7, Louisiana State and Alabama

Most points scored, one team
52, Florida vs. Florida State, 1997

Most passing yards
482, Tim Tebow, Florida vs. Cincinnati, 2010

Most rushing yards
230, Ezekiel Elliot, Ohio State vs. Alabama, 2015

Most receptions
14, Josh Reed, LSU vs. Illinois, 2002

Most receiving yards
239, Josh Reed, LSU vs. Illinois, 2002

Longest touchdown run
92 yards, Ray Brown, Mississippi vs. Texas, 1958

Longest touchdown reception
82 yards, Ike Hilliard, Florida vs. Florida State, 1995

Most tackles
20, Tom Cousineau, Ohio State vs. Alabama, 1978

Fewest yards, team
74, LSU vs. Mississippi, 1960

Widest margin of victory
35 points, Oklahoma (35) vs. LSU (0), 1950

*through the 2015 Sugar Bowl

QUOTES AND ANECDOTES

"You'd better pass."—Alabama defensive lineman Marty Lyons talking to Penn State quarterback Chuck Fusina before the Crimson Tide stuffed the Nittany Lions in a goal-line stand late in the 1979 Sugar Bowl.

"What are the Sugar Bowl passing records? Because I'm gonna break 'em."—Florida quarterback Steve Spurrier before the 1966 game between the Gators and Missouri. Spurrier did throw for a then-record 352 yards, but Florida lost 20–18.

"That was the only one we need."—Georgia coach Vince Dooley on the one completion by quarterback Buck Belue in the 1981 Sugar Bowl. Belue went 1-for-12, his only completion a 7-yard gain in the last two minutes that let the Bulldogs run out the clock in a 17–10 win over Notre Dame to claim the national championship.

Only one Sugar Bowl has ended in a tie. In 1988, Auburn trailed Syracuse 16–13 with one second left. Rather than go for the game-winning touchdown, the Tigers settled for a 30-yard field goal by Win Lyle to tie the game. That was before college football introduced overtime. "We didn't tie them. They tied us," Syracuse quarterback Don McPherson grumbled after the game.

"What's the difference between Notre Dame's football team and Cheerios? Cheerios belong in a bowl."—A joke that a waiter reportedly told Notre Dame coach Lou Holtz in New Orleans before the 1992 Sugar Bowl. The Irish used the quote to fire them up for a 39–28 win over Florida.

45

GLOSSARY

alma mater

Where a person went to college.

campus

The grounds of a school.

conference

A group of schools that joins together to create a league for their sports teams. The Southeast Conference is an example.

favorite

The person or team that is expected to win.

fullback

An offensive player who sometimes runs with the football but is also responsible for blocking.

fumble

When a player with the ball loses possession, allowing the defense the opportunity to recover it.

Heisman Trophy

The award given yearly to the best player in college football.

interception

When a defensive player catches a pass instead of the offensive player.

poll

A survey of people's opinions on a subject. Polls of college football coaches and media are used to rank teams during the season.

safety

A score of two points for the defensive team when the offense is unable to advance the ball out of its own end zone.

FOR MORE INFORMATION

Further Reading
Howell, Brian. *Notre Dame Fighting Irish*. Minneapolis, MN: Abdo Publishing, 2012.

Seidel, Jeff. *Alabama Crimson Tide*. Minneapolis, MN: Abdo Publishing, 2012.

Tebow, Tim, and Nathan Whitaker. *Through My Eyes: A Quarterback's Journey*. Grand Rapids, MI: Zondervan, 2011.

Websites
To learn more about Bowl Games of College Football, visit **booklinks.abdopublishing.com**. These links are routinely monitored and updated to provide the most current information available.

Place to Visit
College Football Hall of Fame
250 Marietta Street NW
Atlanta, Georgia 30313
404-880-4800
www.cfbhall.com
This hall of fame and museum highlights the greatest players and moments in the history of college football. Relocated from South Bend, Indiana, in 2014, it includes multiple galleries, a theater, and an interactive area where fans can test their football skills.

INDEX

Arnold, Claude, 11

Blackledge, Todd, 29, 31
Bowden, Bobby, 37
Bryant, Bear, 9–13, 16–19

Casper, Dave, 18
Cavanaugh, Matt, 23, 25
Clements, Tom, 18

Digby, Fred, 5–7
Dooley, Vince, 22
Dorsett, Tony, 22–23, 25
Dugans, Ron, 35

Garrity, Gregg, 31

Heath, Leon, 11
Hunter, Al, 17

Janikowski, Sebastian, 35
Jones, Gordon, 23

Kendra, Dan, 34

Lockett, Jake, 12

Majors, Johnny, 22, 25
Miller, Warren, 7
Miller-Digby Trophy, 7, 31, 37
Minor, Travis, 34

New Orleans Saints, 21

Parseghian, Ara, 16, 18–19
Paterno, Joe, 27, 29, 31

Stock, Mike, 17
Superdome, 7, 21, 22, 25, 31, 34

Tebow, Tim, 39–41
Thomas, Bob, 17
Thompson, Colonel James M., 5–6
Todd, Richard, 17
Tulane Stadium, 6–7, 15–16, 21, 37

Vessels, Billy, 11
Vick, Michael, 33–34, 37

Walker, Elliot, 23
Walker, Herschel, 28–29, 31
Warner, Curt, 29, 31
Warrick, Peter, 34–35, 37
Weber, Robin, 18–19
Weinke, Chris, 33–35, 37
Wilkinson, Bud, 10

Yowarsky, Walt, 11–12

About the Author

Will Graves grew up wanting to play wide receiver for the NFL's Washington Redskins. He ended up writing about football instead. Graves is an award-winning journalist for the Associated Press. He covers the NFL's Pittsburgh Steelers and University of Pittsburgh football. He now plays quarterback to his son and daughter.